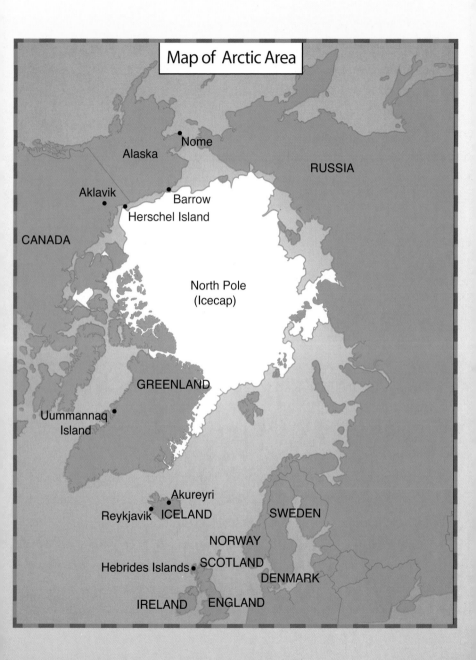

GRADE 5

Lesson 27

WORD COUNT

2,246

GENRE

Biography

LEVEL

See TG or go Online

Harcourt Leveled
Readers Online Database

ISBN-13: 978-0-15-351679-5
ISBN-10: 0-15-351679-8

90000 >

9 780153 516795

Harcourt
SCHOOL PUBLISHERS

A Poppy in the Tundra

The Story of Isobel Wylie Hutchison

by Lisa Moore

illustrated by
Robert Casilla

Harcourt
SCHOOL PUBLISHERS

A Poppy
in the Tundra

The Story of Isobel Wylie Hutchison

by Lisa Moore
illustrated by Robert Casilla

Harcourt
SCHOOL PUBLISHERS

Printed in Mexico

ISBN 10: 0-15-351679-8
ISBN 13: 978-0-15-351679-5

Ordering Options
ISBN 10: 0-15-351215-6 (Grade 5 Advanced Collection)
ISBN 13: 978-0-15-351215-5(Grade 5 Advanced Collection)
ISBN 10: 0-15-358162-X (package of 5)
ISBN 13: 978-0-15-358162-5 (package of 5)

2 3 4 5 6 7 8 9 10   126   12 11 10 09 08 07

Imagine a young woman crouched over a single yellow Arctic poppy, a flower she's never seen before. In her hand is a sketchbook and pencil. On her feet are snowshoes. All around her is frozen tundra. Above her is a clear blue sky where it seems as though the terns scream, "Look! Look!" The flower, like the young woman, is both timid and rugged. Meet Isobel Wylie Hutchison: traveler, botanist, poet, and pioneer.

A Victorian Girl

Isobel Wylie Hutchison grew up near Edinburgh, Scotland, on a large estate cared for by servants and laden with acres of gardens, fields, and woods. Her only friends were her sisters, Nita and Hilda, and her brothers, Walter and Frank. The children were isolated from the outside world, taught at home by tutors. In the summer, they played croquet and tennis on the lawns and hiked in the countryside. In the winter, they went ice-skating and sledding, and the children enjoyed writing and performing plays with the servants as their audience.

At fifteen, Isobel went to a private school in Edinburgh. She wrote in her diary every day, and she loved to read and write poetry. She studied hard and was often at the top of her class, but mostly she kept to herself.

Isobel was born in 1889, near the end of Queen Victoria's reign in England. During this time, young women had few choices in their lives. They were expected to learn needle crafting, drawing, painting, and how to play a musical instrument.

They were discouraged from going to college, and very few women had jobs. Most remained in their parents' homes until they married, and then they had homes with their husbands and raised children.

Two Passions: Poetry & Plants

In the Victorian era, gardening, collecting plants, and pressing flowers were activities that were acceptable for girls. Isobel's father encouraged Isobel to plant and care for her own garden and to keep a record of what she planted. She collected dozens of plants and carefully pressed them flat between sheets of special paper. As Isobel grew older, her interest in botany, the study of plants, and her passion for plant collecting grew to be as strong as her love of poetry.

By 1917, when Isobel was twenty-eight years old, she had already written two books of poetry. Now she wanted to put her knowledge of plants to use—and it was time for her to leave her parents' home. She entered the Studley Horticultural College for Women. (*Horticulture* is another word for gardening.)

Isobel was about ten years older than the other students at Studley College, and at first, she felt that she didn't fit in. However, by the time she graduated, she had gained friends, knowledge, and a new self-confidence.

What Is Botany?

Botany is the scientific study of plants. Some botanists study plant structure, or the parts of plants and how they go together. Other botanists study how plants grow, and still others study plant diseases. All botanists need a good understanding of plant *classification and distribution.*

Papaver Radicatum

Throughout the world, botanists have identified more than 150,000 different plant species. These plants fall into many groups, or families, based on features they have in common. Identifying plants and determining what family they belong to is called plant classification. A plant's *distribution* includes the areas where that plant grows.

Amateur botanists play an important role in the science of botany. Trained botanists can't go everywhere, so they depend on amateurs to send them plants from all over the world. The thousands of plants Isobel Hutchison collected throughout her life were given to universities and botanical societies and contributed to a fuller picture of plant distribution.

A Traveler Is Born

Isobel went from Studley College to a university in London, England. After one year there, she decided to travel. She went to Egypt to see the great pyramids and visited Jerusalem in what is now Israel in the Middle East. She traveled on comfortable cruise ships and passenger trains and stayed in pleasant hotels. She was just a tourist at the time, but she was in preparation for the adventures to come. She set her sights on studying plants in one of the most remote places on earth: Iceland.

Iceland is an island country in the North Atlantic Ocean, located just below the Arctic Circle. The interior of the island is an uninhabited desert of ice and snow. Iceland's first prehistoric settlers were Vikings from Norway and Celts, people from what are now Scotland and Ireland. Before their arrival, no humans had lived there. In modern times, Iceland was, for many decades, a colony of Denmark. It became an independent country seven years before Isobel traveled there.

To prepare for her journey, Isobel walked across each of the Hebrides (HEH•brə•deez) Islands, located off the northwest coast of Scotland, collecting plants along the way. She also studied the languages spoken in Iceland: Danish and Icelandic.

In June 1925, Isobel boarded a steamer ship to Reykjavík (RAY•kyə•vick), the capital of Iceland. There a native guide helped her plan her route. She planned to walk west to east from Reykjavík to the port town of Akureyri (ACK•oo•ree). She would keep close to the coast and follow ancient trails and rough pony tracks.

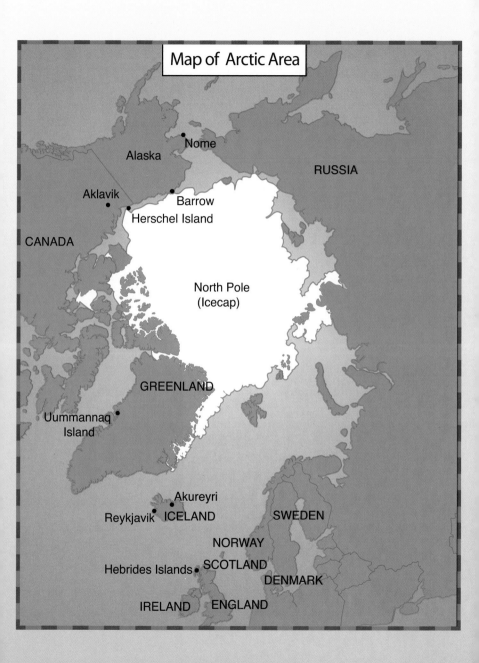

Map of Arctic Area

Nome
Alaska
RUSSIA
Aklavik
Barrow
Herschel Island
CANADA
North Pole
(Icecap)
GREENLAND
Uummannaq
Island
Akureyri
Reykjavik ICELAND SWEDEN
NORWAY
Hebrides Islands SCOTLAND
DENMARK
IRELAND ENGLAND

It may sound grueling to some, but Isobel walked from ten to twenty-five miles a day! Each day's trek brought her to a remote farmhouse or other place of shelter. Although she was an unexpected stranger, she was warmly welcomed at each stop and given a meal

and a warm place to sleep. Each day, her host described what lay ahead and set her on the right path. At more than one spot, a local farmer helped her make a difficult river crossing by pony.

Upon arriving at her next-to-last stop, a village called Nordtunga, Isobel was amazed to find that news of her arrival had traveled ahead of her. The villagers raised a union jack (the flag of the United Kingdom) and prepared a banquet to greet their most unusual guest!

Isobel did not flounder on her quest. After fourteen days, she arrived in Akureyri. She had walked 280 miles (about 450 km)! All along her route, she had collected plants and taken photographs of the plant life, the landscapes, and the people of Iceland. Boarding the ship that would take her back to England, she felt happy, confident, and ready for more adventure.

Next Journey: Greenland

Travel in Greenland would be much more difficult than anything Isobel had experienced in Iceland—but Greenland was now her goal. She had fallen in love with the far north.

Greenland is the largest island in the world. (See the map on page 7.) Only the land along the coast is free of ice. The miles and miles of coastline are toothed with *fjords*, narrow inlets of water between steep, high cliffs. In 1927, when Isobel went there, much of Greenland was unexplored.

Even before Isobel got to Greenland, she had a hurdle to overcome. Greenland was (and still is) part of Denmark. The Danish government in Greenland had a "closed-door policy" to outsiders. They wanted to protect the native Inuit people and their way of life. Only those who served the government and some scientists were allowed to visit. Isobel was only an amateur botanist—but she was a determined one! It took a year, but finally a letter arrived from the Danish Foreign Office inviting her to visit Greenland. In July of 1927, Isobel boarded a sailing ship that took her across the Atlantic to Greenland.

The Inuit People

Inuit means "the people." The Inuit are the large group of native peoples who live in the Arctic region on the coasts of Siberia, Alaska, northern Canada, and Greenland. Although they are spread over a very large region, until recent times all of the Inuit lived in similar ways. They fished and hunted sea mammals and caribou; they made their clothing from animal skins; and they built their homes from stone, driftwood, earth, and grass.

The Inuit in different regions speak different *dialects* of a language that is also called Inuit. Here are some Inuit words. Some of them may sound familiar.

Iglu A dome-shaped shelter made of "bricks" cut from compacted snow. You may know this word as igloo.

Qajaq A covered, single-passenger boat made from sealskin and wood or bone. You may know this word as kayak.

Kamik Inuit boots made from caribou or sealskin, reaching high above the knee.

Umiaq An open boat made of sealskin and bones. Umiaqs are large enough to carry eight to ten people and are propelled by rowing.

Isobel traveled around southern Greenland, walking and hiking, collecting plants, and photographing her surroundings. She learned to live comfortably in a tent. She adopted the warm clothing of the Greenlanders: high sealskin boots called *kamik* and a fur-lined parka. She was carried by Greenlanders around the coast and into fjords in a skin boat called an *umiaq*. In Greenland, she met the great Arctic explorer Knud Rasmussen.

After five months, Isobel returned to Scotland, but she wanted more! Ten months later, she was back in Greenland. She had two goals: to travel north of the Arctic Circle and to understand the lives of the natives. She was invited by Knud Rasmussen to Uummannaq Island. This is a small island in a huge fjord on the west coast of Greenland. The island is just above the Arctic Circle—so Isobel had already reached her first goal!

About 250 people lived on Uummannaq. Ten or twelve were Danish and the rest were Inuit. The captain of Uummannaq's supply boat was away for the winter, so Isobel moved into his small wooden house. The house came with a cook and housekeeper, a native woman named Dorthe.

People who were used to luxury could have been appalled by living in such an environment. However, although Isobel had grown up with servants, she had never been haughty. Still, she was used to having the cooking and cleaning done for her. There was one problem, though. Isobel didn't speak Greenlandic, and Dorthe didn't speak English, but Isobel soon realized that Dorthe didn't need to be told what to do.

Dorthe cooked many kinds of food, lit the woodstove, scrubbed away the constantly collecting soot, and melted glacier ice for water. As the weeks passed, Isobel grew to respect Dorthe and did the chores right along with her. As time passed, they became good friends.

In the meantime, Isobel invested as much time as possible in plant collecting. She needed to work fast since snow would soon cover the plant life and the days would become very short. From November to February, there would be no daylight at all! By the time she left Greenland, Isobel had collected almost 200 different plants.

Through the winter, Isobel stayed in Uummannaq. She joined in the ways of the native villagers and learned the Greenlandic language. She filmed the people going about their daily activities. She didn't just stand back and watch but took part in whatever was happening. When spring came and Isobel boarded the boat that would take her away from Greenland, she felt that she was leaving one home and going back to another.

On to Alaska

In 1933, Isobel went to what is now the state of Alaska. (See map on page 7.) Once again, she set off without a plan. She traveled by ship, train, paddle steamer, and, finally, small airplane to the town of Nome.

In Nome, Isobel was invited to travel on a small boat to Barrow, 500 miles (800 km) away on the north coast. The boat would stop at small native settlements along the way to trade supplies. Because of blizzards and ice, a trip that should have taken five days took five weeks!

From Barrow, Isobel moved on to Herschel Island, in Canada, with a guide named Gus Matik. When Gus and Isobel arrived on Herschel Island, Isobel was amused to learn that the Royal Canadian Mounted Police were looking for her. No one had heard from her since she had left Barrow almost three months before—and those who had thought she was lost had already given up the search for her.

With native guides, Isobel traveled by dogsled from Herschel Island to her last stop, Aklavik. From England, she had covered 13,000 miles (about 21,000 km). She was the first non-native woman to visit the north Alaskan coast. Along the way, she collected more than 700 species of plants.

Isobel made two more voyages to the far north. She returned to Greenland to collect plants, and she explored the Aleutian Islands, which lie in the Bering Sea west of Alaska. She spent her final years in Scotland, reading, writing, and walking the paths she had memorized as a girl. In 1982, she died at the age of ninety-two.

Isobel's Legacy

Isobel Wylie Hutchison never floundered. She wrote poetry, novels, travel books, and magazine articles. She spoke many languages. She was a skilled photographer and filmmaker. Her beautiful watercolor paintings of northern landscapes have been shown in museums and galleries. She gathered thousands of plants that are still part of botanical collections. Perhaps Isobel's greatest achievement was that everywhere she went she made friends, each one as precious and unique to her as a wildflower in the snow.

Think Critically

1. Why did Isobel Wylie Hutchison choose a life of travel and exploration rather than a typical "Victorian" life?

2. Based on what you have read, write a summary of the Inuit people and their culture.

3. In your own words, describe the science of botany.

4. Why do you think the author chose Isobel as a subject?

5. How was Isobel like a "poppy in the tundra"?

 **Social Studies**

More on Greenland Do research on the Internet or using another library resource to learn more about the history of Greenland. Summarize your findings in a paragraph or two.

School-Home Connection With an adult family member, explore your neighborhood for plant life. Try to identify as many plants as you can and make a list. You may wish to check a plant guidebook for any plants you don't know.

Word Count: 2,246 (with graphic 2,275)

GRADE 5

Lesson 27

WORD COUNT

2,246

GENRE

Biography

LEVEL

See TG or go Online

 Harcourt Leveled
Readers Online Database

ISBN-13: 978-0-15-351679-5
ISBN-10: 0-15-351679-8

9 780153 516795

SCHOOL PUBLISHERS

Advanced Books Collection
Grade 5

5 copies of
A Poppy in the Tundra: The Story of
Isobel Wylie Hutchinson

Harcourt
SCHOOL PUBLISHERS

Visit *The Learning Site!*
www.harcourtschool.com

ISBN-13: 978-0-15-358162-5
ISBN-10: 0-15-358162-X

flysheet 9997-82630-2